The Bright Side

Written & Illustrated by

Destany Lytle

About the Book

This is not a true memoir, as I do not highlight every stage of my life. I chose short stories connected to lessons learned. My inspiration for writing this book is to bring children out of generational and emotional poverty.

This is not a traditional book in the sense that I DON'T want them to just read it. I want them to experience it! Every section has an activity for them to take part in. Through these activities I want them to discover what brings them joy, what they can do when they experience hard times, and who the people are that will help them accomplish their goals. I want them to draw, color, and design in this book. I want the book to become as personal to them as a journal.

I have titled it a photographic memoir, but in truth, it simply is creative chaos.

To every child...

You have the power to choose the direction you will take in life. You can be or have anything that you want, if you are willing to work for it. Remember, everything takes time, and of all the wonders in the world you are the greatest.

Destany Lytle

GYPSY BEGINNING

A Journey with Destany!

As a child, my back yard had waterfalls, deserts, rattlesnakes, and bighorn sheep. This would ordinarily seem far-fetched, but I lived on a bus. It was not extravagant by any means. In fact, it had one bedroom, a kitchenette, a bathroom, and a couch. My Mamaw, Papaw, Mom, twin sister, and I all lived together. Ironically, it never felt crowded.

Outside my window, the landscape was always changing. Sometimes I would wake up, and Papaw would say, "I feel like going to Arizona." So that is exactly what we would do. Mamaw always said we had a gypsy soul. Truly, we were nomads. We traveled the United States this way.

Little did I know that I, too, was changing. I was evolving. A passion for adventure and sense of wonder for the world around me flowed through my veins.

Join me on my journey of discovery!

While you read and enjoy the adventures of my life,
I challenge you to make adventures of your own.

A MISUNDERSTANDING

A note from Destany -

Part of the nomadic lifestyle is being able to adapt to any location. Having the bus made the experience like camping. A caravan of my extended family with their children would follow the bus in their vehicles.

At one point in my life when I was about six years old, we were living by a river in Arizona while my folks were on the hunt for a home to rent. During that time, my family found odd jobs, and I remember much of my life spent on farms. We would pick blueberries, pull weeds from gardens, or any other work available. We survived by our willingness to take hard jobs.

Even as children, we were expected to help labor, too. To be honest, I may have eaten the fruit I was supposed to pick! Thankfully, two days later my family landed part time jobs.

Never in my life did I dream that a nice family outing to the mountains of Arizona would result in me being chased by my own Aunt who carried a knife. It all started two days prior to the outing. My family planned to go hiking up to Antelope mountain. My twin sister, Felisha and I weren't too keen on going, so Papaw said we could hunt for gold while on the trip.

That's all the encouragement I needed. I began dreaming of buying a mansion for my family. For myself, I wanted a small treehouse. It was going to have a skylight, a telescope, a book shelf, soft fluffy rugs, a bed, and a refrigerator complete with snacks. I would live there forever.

The day of the trip, I was ready to go! I chatted with Felisha about my plans and listened to hers. We were certain that we would find gold. I took in the vast mountain range. Hues of brown covered the land. Green cacti breathed color into the landscape. I remember listening to the crunch the ground made as gravel rolled under my feet with every step. I also remember it being very hot.

Not long into the hike, I had taken the lead of the expedition in my quest for gold. I didn't realize that I had gotten too far ahead. Mom called out to me, "Destany...."

Upon hearing my name, I spun around to see what she wanted. As I did so, the rest of Mom's words were lost. I felt a sting in my right wrist and looked down to see a cactus lodged in my skin. A thousand needles pricked me at once! I tried to pull it off to no avail. I only pricked my finger and a barb of the cactus stuck in it.

I called my mom for help. She too tried to get it out, but could not. The next thing I know, I see that my Aunt is coming towards me with a very large knife.

Panic. I began to scream. There were houses not far from us and people began to stare. I called out for help. Mom grabbed my arm. Being six years old, I knew in my heart of hearts that the only thing left to do was to cut off my arm.

"Please don't cut off my arm!" I begged. "Help!"

A helicopter flew over and I wished they would scoop me up. Felisha ran to my rescue, and began to plead for them to leave me alone. My Uncle David had to carry her away as she tried to keep them from cutting off my arm. In the middle of all the hysteria, my Aunt had wrapped the knife in a towel. "Destany calm down! We're not going to cut off your arm. Look at your wrist."

I braved a glance. It was gone! They had plucked the cactus off without me even noticing. I was so happy! I saw little red bumps where the cactus had stuck to me. I smiled through tears. Then, I began to giggle, knowing I would still be able to climb in the future.

Mom and the rest of the family decided to call off the trip. I didn't find any gold, nor did we make it to the summit.

When we arrived at home, I hugged Papaw. I told him how Aunt Sherry tried to cut off my arm and how mom just let it happen. He laughed, noticing that I still had two arms. My shoulders dropped when I told him I didn't find any gold. He wrapped me in a bear hug and said I was rich in the way it counted most.

In all my years, I have seen numerous precious minerals. None of them compare to the beauty of the light I find in my Papaw's eyes. Nor does it compare to the value of life that he and the rest of my family has provided for me.

ACTIVITY

Let's exercise your imagination! On the next page <u>design your own tree house.</u>
Draw a picture of what it would look like.

Believe In Yourself

A note from Destany –

My mom bought a house in Corning, Arkansas. I was nine years old, and close to my second-grade year in 2004,. Growing up on a bus, public school was new to me. It went okay, but there was one kid who always gave me a hard time. His name was Dillion.

"You can't do it!" Dillion screamed at me.

He was a foot taller than me, and the strongest boy in our class. He had brown hair, and freckles sprinkled on his face. His cheeks were the color of fire, which matched his mood.

I looked up at the tall oak tree. Branches stuck out in every direction. "Yes, I can!" I insisted. Hearing the argument, a crowd gathered around us.

Earlier that morning, Dillion had boasted in class that he could climb any tree. As it turns out, he couldn't climb this one. The first branch was out of his reach.

Noticing the group of students, the teacher started towards us. I knew it was now or never, and climbing was second nature to me. I leaped toward the trunk of the tree. Kicking off the side with my left foot, I threw myself upwards. With both arms outstretched, I latched onto the first branch. I wrapped my legs onto the branch too, then pulled myself up on the side closest to the trunk. I stood up on the branch and smiled. Then I quickly started climbing for the top.

By the time I made it to the summit, the teacher had arrived. Half of the kids had quickly retreated as soon as they saw her coming. I hugged the tree trunk tight and closed my eyes. I believed that if I stood still enough she would not spot me.

I dared a peek just in time to see Dillion point up at me. My teacher's eyes followed his finger. When she spotted me, her face became ghostly pale. Her mouth dropped open. In a tone more frightened than angry, she yelled, "Get down from there now!"

When I touched the ground, everyone was gone except for Dillion and the teacher.

"Well what do you have to say for yourself?" She demanded.

Dillion waited for my response with a smirk. He knew I was in trouble.

"I climbed the tree," I said proudly.

A moment of silence, then my teacher did something unexpected. She chuckled. That much was obvious to her already. With her infinite kindness and grace, she sensed this was something bigger. She dismissed Dillion to recess. Without me disclosing a single detail, she deciphered what had happened. I neither confirmed nor denied her hypothesis. I just waited for my punishment.

To my surprise, I did not get in trouble. She talked to me about safety and told me that she didn't want to see me get hurt. She then made it clear I was not allowed to climb trees (at school).

This event taught me that sometimes others will try to tell you that you are incapable of doing something simply because they cannot do it themselves. I also learned others DO NOT get to decide what I am capable of accomplishing. That is a decision we must make for ourselves.

ACTIVITY

Journal Entry: Think of a time in your life that someone told you they didn't believe you could accomplish something. How did that make you feel? How did you respond? (Remember you CAN DO anything you set your mind to.)

Journal:

_____

_____

_____

_____

_____

_____

_____

_____

_____

_____

_____

_____

_____

_____

_____

_____

_____

ACCOMPLISHMENT PAGE

Fill your page with accomplishments you have made. Let it serve as a reminder of the things you have achieved in the past, so you can overcome obstacles and accomplish more in the future.

You can Do Hard things!

Keep Climbing

Be Strong.

Never give up.

SWITCHING PLACES

"I have an idea!"

Felisha ran up to me in our bedroom. She seemed surprisingly happy considering that just a few moments ago, she was on the verge of tears.

"What is your idea?" I inquired.

"Well I was thinking about how you have a math test today... aaaaaaaand you know I have a science test. What if we switched places?"

I stared at her for a moment. I knew this was the wrong thing to do, but suddenly I wasn't worried about my math test. I never did poorly in math, I just had to work a lot harder than Felisha did. It's as if she understood some secret language of numbers. She always finished her math homework with a breeze. I was the same way in science. My wonder about the world around me and the hidden processes in which it functions helped me to excel in science.

So, we devised our plan. I wore her favorite shirt and she wore mine. We thought of the difficulties we might face, like being sure to answer to the right name. That wouldn't be too hard. We were used to answering each other's names. Most people confused us often, so it had become a habit to answer to Felisha or Destany. The next obstacle was ensuring that I talked to her friend group and she talked to mine that morning at school. We always stayed together at recess, so that wouldn't be hard.

We reviewed the plan on the bus ride to school. Once there, I walked to her homeroom and she walked to mine. I sat down in Felisha's assigned seat. Thankfully, they all had name tags. The teacher wasted no time in starting the test.

"Clear your desk of everything except for a pencil," she instructed.

My heart raced. She began to pass out the test. The click of her shoes was edging closer and closer to me. Click, click, click... one more test given. Click, click, click... another test given.

Finally, she made it to my desk, or rather, Felisha's desk. She placed the paper down, then walked right past me. I wrote Felisha's name on the paper. The test was easy. It was about patterns of weather. I looked at each question and knew the answer to each one. I went to work answering questions. I made sure to pause and think about some of them a little longer like I was hoping Felisha was doing on mine. As I neared the last question, I started to feel guilty.

After the tests were collected, I raised my hand. Click, click, click, the teacher started toward me. She stood over me for a minute. I found my courage. "I'm not Felisha. I'm Destany. Felisha and I switched places."

The weight of my words settled on her skin. She instructed everyone to take out their readers and turn to page twenty-one. Every eye was on me, but they did as they were asked. "Come with me," she said.

My homeroom teacher's class was about fifteen feet from Felisha's classroom. As soon as we exited the threshold, I saw Felisha and my homeroom teacher. We met in the middle. The four of us – two teachers looking down at twin girls. Felisha and I looked at the floor. We must have confessed at the exact same time!

In the end, they called our mom. They were surprised that we had switched places, but in their good humor and grace, they let us keep the grade that the other twin scored. We both made A's. Guilt was our true punishment. While I ended up with a good grade, I didn't feel good about the choice I had made. I knew I had lost some of my teacher's trust, and she meant the world to me.

As my Dad always says, "There are no shortcuts in life worthwhile. We have to work hard for the things we want."

ACTIVITY

Circle your favorite subject in school.

ART	MUSIC	WRITING	READING
HISTORY	SPORTS	MATH	SCIENCE

Look up a career related to this subject!

_____

Tag me in the career that interests you!

#journeywithdestany

Kindness

A note from Destany –

Did you know kindness increases a chemical in your body that makes you feel happy? In addition, when someone sees you being kind it can inspire them to carry out acts of kindness, too. Kindness is literally contagious.

Many of my fondest memories involve my mother. I remember when I was a little girl, we lived for a short period of time in Corning, Arkansas. We always did our grocery shopping once a month at the local Walmart. Outside the entrance were five soda machines and she stopped to get Felisha and me a soda. After she bought us one each, she put another quarter in the machine. Felisha and I wanted to push the button for another soda, but she instructed us not to. She filled every machine up with quarters.

"These are for someone else," she said with a smile.

"Who?" Felisha and I were curious.

"I don't know, but just imagine when some kid, much like you, comes along and pushes one of those buttons. To their surprise, the machine will start to rumble and then *bam!* Out pops a free soda. I believe that would make someone else very happy. Don't you?" Mom asked.

"Yes, ma'am," we both agreed.

Of all the things my mother did in kindness, this is my favorite. I realize what made it so special is that she never saw who received the sodas. She didn't want credit. She did this small act of kindness out of the goodness of her heart.

Kindness was its own reward. All my life my family was never wealthy. However, this never stopped them from helping others in need. Witnessing these moments ascertained my view that one of the most important qualities a person can have is kindness. Kindness does not have to be done monetarily, meaning you don't need money to show kindness.

I have asked a group of students to share their ideas of ways people can show kindness. Kids have the power to change the world! One of the ways to accomplish this is through acts of kindness. Here is what some of the difference makers in my community had to say.

Kindness Rockstars

- "If you see trash in the parking lot, pick it up and throw it away." Addison Henderson Age 11

- When speaking to adults, show respect by saying yes ma'am, no ma'am, and yes sir, no sir." Harley Knight, age 12

- "Give someone a compliment." Brooks Price & Jonathan Perez, ages 11

- "Hold the door for someone." Easton Warden, age 11

- "Leave a positive and encouraging note. Leave it for a stranger or for someone you know to find." Leslie Guthery, age 15

- "Clean the house without being told to. This will make it easier on your mom throughout the day." Ethan Williford, age 12

- "Do what you can to help others." Summer Dickerson, age 12

- "Say "good job" to the opposing team in the basketball game." Kaylie Barger, age 12

- "You can simply thank people, like the janitors or the bus drivers, because they sometimes get overlooked." June McFarland, age 11

- "Instead of throwing away clothes that are too small or that you don't want anymore, you can donate them." Sammy Malone, age 12

- "Help your parents carry in groceries." Kaleb Cox, age 12

- "Give unexpected gifts." Johnathan Huckabee, age 12

- "If you see another student who is lost, tell them how to get where they're trying to go." Jobe Garrett, age 11

- "A simple "Hi!" can mean the world to someone." Dillon Holt, age 12

- "Help a kid read." Ryleigh Piety, age 12

- "If you see someone fall, help them up." Avery Swafford, age 12

- "Always be a good teammate by encouraging each other." Carley Piety, age 12

- "If you get change, put it in the tip box." Maleki Rodriguez, age 12

- "Help others. One day you might need help too." Jayden Price, age 11

- "Give food or drink to someone in need." Sawyer Delargy, age 12

- "Pray for people that you know need it." Kadence Pulley, age 12

- "If someone looks upset, ask them if they're okay or if they need help." London Porterfield, age 11

- "Make someone a card and write something from the heart on it. Waylon Altom, age 12

- "Help your parents cook, and with chores around the house." Emma Vanwinkle, age 11

- "Help your teacher with classroom jobs." Breeze Barnhouse, age 11

- "Give someone a high-five." Isaiah Rodriguez, age 12

- "Clean up the school playground." Landon Windland, age 12

- "Surprise someone with a gift. It can be homemade." Logan Tate, age 12

- "Tie a little kid's shoes for them." Brooks Price, age 11

- "Play with someone during recess who doesn't have anyone to play with." Brantley Langle, age 12

- "When someone is sad, just listen to what they have to say." Marlee Goetzman, age 11

ACTIVITY

Tag me in your ideas by using the hashtag: #journeywithdestany

Directions: Write down ways that you do or can do kindness to others in the box below. Ask your parent(s) or guardian to post your ideas to social media to inspire others to do the same. Remember, money is not required to show kindness.

Kindness

Fireflies

A note from Destany –
Did you know the "firefly" or "lightning bug" is actually a bioluminescent beetle?
The flashing we see is a form of communication and sometimes even a lure.

When I first moved to Missouri, I found the endless farm fields to be less than beautiful.

Having grown up around the mountains, I missed the overlooks where I could sit on a summit and see how water carved out entire canyons, like a time capsule before my eyes.

In Moark, Missouri, it was so different – everything was flat. I could see for miles, but the view never changed. Even so, I soon learned that Missouri becomes magical once a year, and it happens in the month of August.

Lemon slices danced between ice cubes in a glass of sweet tea, while clean sheets billowed in the breeze on the clothesline. The air was thick. I watched the horizon and waited patiently, watching The Great Artist busy at work. Blue skies were transformed into shades of purple. Strokes of crimson and pink stretched out in waves. The sunset was the last preliminary show before the main event.

A living light show was waiting for its turn.

As darkness blanketed the sky, the magic began. At first, you could only see one or two, then, in an explosion, they were everywhere. Green, orange, and yellow lights were flashing through the night. Fireflies filled the air.

My siblings and I would take mason jars and see who could catch the most. We would hold the jar up close to our face, and admire them. Stars shone bright above our heads. Darkness was chased away by thousands of blinking fireflies that surrounded us in joy.

In all the states I have lived in, I have never seen as many fireflies as those I found in the farm fields of Moark, Missouri.

ACTIVITY

Tag me on social media when you go firefly hunting! #journeywithdestany

Firefly Hunting

Materials Needed:

- Plastic or glass jar
- Grass
- Paper towel

Instructions:

1. Punch small holes into the lid of your jar. This allows oxygen into the container, which the fireflies need to survive.

2. Place a small amount of grass in your jar.

3. Wet your paper towel and place it at the bottom of the jar.

Best Time of Year to Catch fireflies

The best time to hunt fireflies is typically in the summer. However, this depends on where you live. You can always Google to find the best season in your area for hunting fireflies.

Thoughts:

_____

_____

_____

_____

Build A Boat

We were bored!

Sometimes in desperate situations such as this, siblings will call a truce and agree to spend time together to hopefully get rid of the boredom. Felisha and I went to our older brother Little Bruce. We called him Little Bruce because his dad is also named Bruce.

"Let's go outside," I suggested.

Immersed in his own boredom, he agreed. So, we headed out to find an adventure.

After four straight days of rain, it finally had subsided. The ground had a rich earthy smell and droplets of water hugged every object in sight. There was a glow about the property that can only be provided by fresh rain. A wide irrigation ditch stretched along the back yard used to provide water to the farm fields. Usually it is dry, but due to the recent rain it was now roaring! The water was high and too swift to cross on foot. This inspired a truly wonderful idea.

We decided to make a boat.

First, we would need to make a trip to the edge of the property to find the metal junk pile. When we got there, the three of us searched around. We looked at an old hood and a huge barrel, but nothing was quite right. Then, Bruce spotted it. Our beautiful boat. It was the shell of an old refrigerator, and it was more than long enough to hold all three of us.

Our next step was to ensure it was waterproof. There were a few small holes rusted into it. Little Bruce found some old silicone that had not been entirely used up, and filled the holes. We smoothed the silicone over the edges and let it dry. Then we were ready to sail our boat!

We dragged the refrigerator to the edge of the creek. Bruce had found a long stick to help steer the boat. We slowly eased it into the water and held our breath, hoping it would float.

It did! We climbed in.

Instantly, it began to fill with water. We quickly got back out to figure out how to stop the leak. Having used up the silicone, Felisha found buckets. Our new plan was to empty water while Little Bruce paddled us across.

Round two. We loaded into the boat, and Felisha and I went to work emptying it of water. We scooped like crazy! All that could be heard for miles was the scraping of our buckets against the metal of the boat.

"Watch it!" Little Bruce suddenly shouted. We had unintentionally splashed him with our hard work, and now water dripped from his hair.

While we kept the boat from sinking, Bruce pushed it slightly against the current, angling it toward the opposite bank.

We made it across the creek! In the end, every single one of us was sopping wet and cold, but what fun we had!

Tag me in a picture of your boat! #journeywithdestany

ACTIVITY

Design Your Own Boat

Materials Needed:

- Aluminum foil
- Popsicle sticks
- Pennies (for weight)

Directions:

Be innovative! The design is completely up to you. After it is completed, use the pennies to see how much weight it can hold.

Challenge:

Invite your family to also create their own boat – see whose boat can hold the most weight.

Thoughts:

_____

_____

_____

_____

_____

_____

_____

The Other Side of Fear

In 2008, I had to make one of the hardest decisions of my life. It started with a summer visit to see my Dad after we had been away from him for three years.

We had been living in California during this time of separation, and I remember how much I missed him, and how every day I would look for him. Anytime I saw a convertible, I thought dad could be driving that car because he was the coolest. I would also look for aviator sunglasses, because that's what Dad always wore. After three years, Mom returned to Arkansas, so we had the opportunity to see Dad again.

We were going to spend a month of summer vacation with him. Spending time with Dad was great. Every weekend we visited places like Petit Jean State Park, War Eagle Mountain, and Blanchard Springs Caverns. We had movie nights and watched John Wayne. It was during this time I decided I wanted to live with my Dad.

After this decision, my life was bliss and torture. In my greatest moments of joy, I wanted to tell my twin and mom all about them. Then I would feel guilty I could be happy here, while they were somewhere else. They had gone back to California and I hadn't heard from them.

It was during this time that I experienced the highest level of anxiety. My seventh-grade year of school I went to several doctors because I began to break out in hives. Typically, these are associated with allergies, but in my case the doctors said it was caused by stress. I also began to grit my teeth while I slept. This too, was a result of stress, and it caused bones to grow in my mouth.

In moments when I experienced happiness, guilt would creep in. I felt the choice I made was selfish. Then, the worst of the stress would occur. Have you ever had your breath knocked out of you? If you have, then you might be able to grasp the feeling in which I am about to describe. It happened often to me. I would be so happy, but then I would remember the choice I had made and how it made my family feel. It was as if a ghost punched me in my stomach. I would stop breathing and feel like I would choke to death. There was also a pressure on my chest as if all of earth's gravity focused its attention on me. My heart would race.

During these moments, I would go to my room and hide. I didn't want people to know I was struggling. I share this information because I have learned that stress is not only emotional, it is physical. It is an unseen monster that can wreak havoc on your body and cause physical pain. I share this story to point out the importance of seeking support from a trusted adult. If you feel this way, consider talking with a teacher or counselor.

STRESS

Imagine there are three people who are asked to carry a load of rocks up a mountain. One person is given a backpack, another is given a thin plastic bag, and the final one is asked to use only their hands. Who do you think is going to be able to handle this task the easiest?

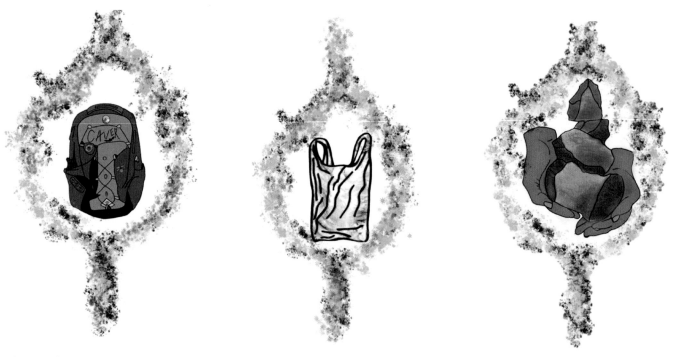

The rocks represent stress, and the person with the backpack is going to fare better than the rest to carry them. We can <u>NOT</u> measure someone's stress against our own because we are all supplied with different tools to carry that load.

The summit of the mountain represents our goals and dreams. We will always be weighted down with stress. In addition to stress, we will face obstacles to reach the top.

Resources and coping strategies represent the tools with which we carry or alleviate the weight of stress.

GOAL SETTING

Growing up, my family couldn't afford many things beyond what was considered "needs," like spare blankets. There was one for each bed and that was it. Typically, we had to share a bed with a sibling. Usually, the person I shared with would roll up in the blanket, and I would be cold all night. I would dream of the day when I had my own house. It would have several comforters for each bed, plus an unnecessary amount of big, fluffy throw blankets.

I started thinking of my future at a very young age. For any "extras," I knew I would have to pay for them myself. In fact, I had an old composition notebook in which I glued pictures from magazines. I was twelve when I made it. Those pictures represented what I wanted my future to look like. It had pictures of a Jeep, a cabin, a teacher, a pretty smile, and blankets.

My dream was to become a teacher, live in a cabin, drive a Jeep, get braces, and, of course, to have a house full of blankets.

During my senior year of high school, a reporter came to interview my twin sister and me. She asked about my plans for the future, and I shared them with her. In the next four years, I did every single thing I told her I would do.

At the age of 21, my husband and I built our cabin. At 22, I became a teacher at Midland Elementary School. At 23, I purchased a Jeep Wrangler.

At 25, I paid for myself to get invisible aligners for my teeth through Smile Direct Club. Also, today, you could walk into my house, and in the hallway closet you will find a ridiculous amount of blankets.

It may sound simple, but I managed to accomplish it all by working three jobs through college. I also had help from my husband, family, and friends. It wasn't easy. I had to struggle a lot before I managed to reach the summit of my scrapbook goals.

The best part is, I'm not finished yet! I have new goals and dreams I am working towards. One day, I may decide I want something completely different. My point in sharing this, is that ANYTHING is possible, so long as you are willing to work for it.

Adapted from EMOTIONAL POVERTY by Ruby K. Payne, Ph.D., pp. 18-19

ACTIVITY
I want to see your plans for the future! Use the hashtag #journeywithdestany.

CREATE YOUR OWN FUTURE STORY!

PHOTO COLLAGE: A piece of art made from sticking various pictures together.

Consider the following:

- What do you want your house to look like?

- What is your dream job?

- What is your next educational step to acquiring your dream job (graduate high school, graduate college with associates, bachelors, etc...)?

- What are your hobbies?

- What is something you would love to do even if you didn't get paid for it?

- Will you make a lot of money?

After considering the questions above, I want you to cut out pictures from a magazine or print your own pictures that represent the answer to these questions. Glue them together on one sheet of paper to create a photo collage.

Thoughts:

_____
_____
_____
_____
_____
_____
_____
_____
_____

Adapted from EMOTIONAL POVERTY by Ruby K. Payne, Ph.D., pp. 148-149

POSITIVE SELF-TALK

Self-talk is the dialogue we have internally.
There is both positive self-talk and negative self-talk.

Self-talk plays a major role in our life. If we have negative self-talk, it will allow doubt to creep in. It will make us question changes we want to make in our life, or convince us that we are unable to try something new. Get rid of negative self-talk, because you are amazing!

The good news is that if you predominantly use negative self-talk, you can change that! Start practicing positive self-talk. After repetitive use, it will become a habit. Watch how quickly your life can change from having a positive mindset.

TRANSFORM YOUR SELF-TALK FROM NEGATIVE TO POSITIVE		
Negative self-talk	CHANGE TO	Positive self-talk
"I can't do this."	CHANGE TO	"With practice, I CAN do this."
"Why would I even try?"	CHANGE TO	"I'm going to learn something new!"
"You're not as good as they are."	CHANGE TO	"The only person I'm competing with is who I was yesterday."

Make your own transformation statements!

NEGATIVE	TO	POSITIVE
	CHANGE TO	
	CHANGE TO	
	CHANGE TO	
	CHANGE TO	
	CHANGE TO	
	CHANGE TO	
	CHANGE TO	

Lighthouse Adults

A lighthouse serves as a guide for ships at sea. Life is like sailing on the water. Most of the time the waves are calm and the sky is clear. However, there are also seasons of storms. The lighthouse serves as a constant guide.

A lighthouse adult is an individual who encourages, supports, and guides you. I would like to recognize my lighthouse adults and thank them. They played a major role in supporting me and have positively impacted my life.

PAIGE ATKISON CATT was my second-grade teacher. She showed me how to love and demonstrate kindness. I had her for one year. She had kept pictures of my sister and me. She also saved samples of my school and art work. My senior year of high school she found me on Facebook, and mailed all the items she had saved. She still checks on me through social media, and encourages me.

Mrs. Catt taught me life skills like how to cope when something doesn't go my way. As a child, I would be devastated if I didn't do well on an assignment. I also did not handle corrections well. I was never defiant, but I felt like making a mistake made me a bad person. The truth is, as she pointed out, we all make mistakes in life. That is what makes us human. In addition, when we don't do well at a task, it just means we have room to grow. It is a good thing! Once we master one skill, then it's time to learn a new one.

KEITH BRIGANCE was my seventh-grade social studies teacher. Mr. Brigance gave all of his students nicknames. My nickname was Marsha Brady, because I had long brown hair. When I would get off task he would say, "Marsha, Marsha, Marsha." Without another word I would go back to work.

Mr. B, as we called him, always greeted his students with a smile. He took the time to learn our interests. Every morning before class started we would talk about the Duke, John Wayne, or any other fifties icon I had an interest in. He would talk about real world concerns. He met every question I had with an eagerness to answer or provided me with the tools by which to answer them. I remember the day before my birthday I joked that he should bring our class chocolate chip cookies. The next day, he did! We also played my favorite trivia game. It was my favorite birthday of all. He is, to this day, one of the main reasons I became a teacher. I remember how he was always happy to see us. I strive to create this type of learning environment for my students as well.

LARRY MCBRIDE was my AP Biology teacher. He is one of the coolest people that you could ever meet. He would always connect an epic adventure story to our lessons! He could do Elvis impersonations and other famous individuals. We loved it! He even let me conduct my own research in the lab.

One of my favorite memories is when we cultured a colony of fruit flies to study physical traits. The fruit fly population would grow rapidly. We would have to transfer colonies from one container to the next. The way to do this is to anesthetize the flies. Once that is accomplished, I needed to transfer them into a fresh container. Well, one time I didn't hold the chemical over the container as long as needed. The result was when I went to transfer them about a hundred fruit flies made their escape. Maybe this sounds like no big deal, but as I said, their population grows rapidly. They ended up traveling all the way from the Biolab to the school cafeteria. The lunch ladies were rightfully upset. The flies had taken over the kitchen. In desperation, they had to break code and hang fly ribbons from the ceiling. They are the long sticky pieces of tape. After about a month of combat they managed to get it under control. Mr. McBride never sold me out. He also let me continue helping with the study of fruit flies. Mr. McBride was the kind of teacher who kept the content rigorous, yet fun. He captured the wonders of the world in his lessons.

JOHN PARKS was my tenth grade English teacher. He, too, had a joyful presence. When you walked in the room, you knew it was going to be an awesome day. He made everything fun. In addition, Mr. Parks never yelled at his students. He remained calm and encouraging. One of my favorite things about Mr. Parks was his ability to comfort students when they were going through a hard time. He never ignored when someone was upset. Whether it be another teacher or student he would check on them. Mr. Parks is the very definition of a lighthouse individual. I loved going to his class. He had an awesome sense of humor and the ability to make you smile. He chose lessons that developed empathy. Mr. Parks taught me to make learning fun. In addition, he taught me that we make a world of difference by the simple act of listening to how another person is feeling without judging their situation. He was a constant source of encouragement.

MARY COMSTOCK was my college instructor for several different literacy courses. She went above and beyond that, too. Mrs. Comstock became my advisor. Instructors are all given a list of students to advise on what classes to take and to answer questions students might have. I was not on her list, but she helped me anyway. What I loved most about her classes was listening to her read. When Mrs. Comstock reads, it is as if the words come to life. They float on the air, then settle on your skin, soaking into

meaning. I never fully appreciated poetry until I took her class. She presented literature that challenged my way of thinking. From her teaching, my beliefs and values evolved. I gave more grace to others. I spent less time making judgments, and more time on making self-assessments.

One day Mrs. Comstock and I discussed my love of Lucille Ball. It wasn't a long conversation and I soon forgot about it. Then, at random, she brought a Lucille Doll from the episode "The Ballet" on the *I Love Lucy* show. It meant the world to me! As I write this, I am looking at my *I love Lucy* collection and I can't help but smile. "The Ballet" is my favorite episode of all time. I dearly cherish the gift and the lady who gave it to me.

DENNIS DEVINE was another one of my college instructors. Mr. Devine is an individual who encourages his students. His courses were always enlightening as well as entertaining. He had a wonderful sense of humor. I remember the first course I had with him as my instructor was oral communications. It is the equivalent of speech class. We would have to give several speeches. At the end of the speech, the floor would be opened for feedback from other students, and to my horror, the class would rate you on a scale of one to ten on how well they thought you did! On our first day Mr. Devine addressed the class, "No one has ever died giving a speech. You will all be fine." I quickly learned one of my peers was the equivalent of Simon Cowell. He always had negative things to say back to the speakers. Once he looked a girl straight in the face and said, "You said the word "like" twenty-three times during your speech."

The first week I had to give a speech introducing myself to the class. I managed to get to the end of my speech, but then I had an anxiety attack. I couldn't control my breathing. In fact, I couldn't catch a breath. It was awful. I waited for "Simon" to give me a negative comment. To my surprise the negative comment never came. At the end of class, Mr. Devine pulled me aside. He said, "Destany I know I said no one has ever died while giving a speech, but I thought today you might be the first." We laughed so much at his joke. After I finished the first speech, it became easier. I actually learned I was a great public speaker.

Mr. Devine taught me to be confident. He gave me critical skills that served me well in my job at Blanchard Springs Caverns and as an educator. He also helped advise me in college. I attribute a large part of my success to both Mr. Devine and Mrs. Comstock. They made a difference in my life.

To these six individuals, thank you for everything.
I hope to follow in your footsteps and help others as you have helped me.

ACTIVITY

Directions: Think of your favorite coach or teacher. What makes them your favorite? Write a letter to let them know you appreciate them.

Adapted from EMOTIONAL POVERTY by Ruby K. Payne, Ph.D., pp. 50-51

EMOJI EMOTIONS

Sometimes it's hard to express how we feel. I want you to be able to put into words what you are feeling. That way when you are talking with someone, you can help voice what you are experiencing.

ACTIVITY

Directions:

Cut out and glue the picture next to what word you think it goes best with.
You are entitled to your feelings. You are strong and capable.

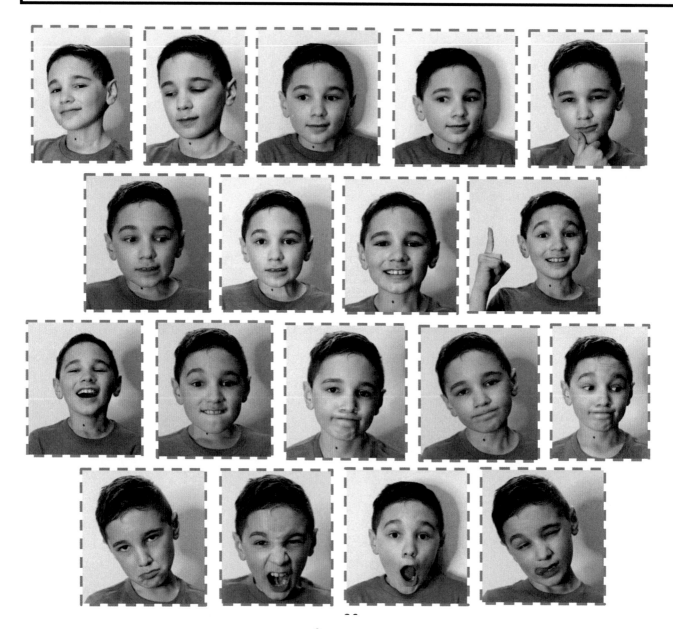

Emotion	Emoji
Joyful	
Sad	
Hostile	
Guilty	
Disappointed	
Proud	

Emotion	Emoji
Confident	
Shy	
Cautious	
Shocked	
Afraid	
Overwhelmed	

SELF LOVE

One of the things that concerns me most is how harshly people tend to judge themselves. As an educator, I ask my students at the beginning of the year to write down three things they admire about themselves. It is on a sheet of paper that no one else will see but me. It is heartbreaking because they all struggle to come up with even one answer. I do not believe it is because they hate who they are, but it is because self-love is seen as selfish.

Next, I hand them another sheet of paper asking them to write down three things they enjoy doing. Their responses to this question are always immediate! An example of what one student wrote is below.

1. "I like to draw."
2. "Spend time with my friends."
3. "Play basketball."

From this I learned all the items she listed were admirable qualities about this herself. She was an excellent artist, a great friend to her peers, and an athlete. Throughout the year, this student showed me her artwork. If there was an away game I missed, she would tell me how it went and what she did in the game! She would also come to me if she was concerned about a friend. This is an example of just one student, but the process applies to every student I have taught in my five years of teaching.

It is okay to celebrate your strengths and weaknesses. They are what makes you unique! It is not selfish to recognize the qualities that are admirable in you. You are amazing! You should admire yourself. If you didn't, then what would you have to be proud of? I know you would quickly be able to celebrate what someone else has done. Make time for yourself. Celebrate who you are. Celebrate the qualities you bring into the word around you.

Just because you admire something about yourself, doesn't mean you are claiming perfection. There will always be room for growth. The only person we should compare ourselves to is who we were yesterday.

ACTIVITY

Directions: Written in the Glow & Grow chart below is the example I shared on p. 29. Now it's your turn! Write three things in the "Glow" column that you admire about yourself, then write how you can improve and "Grow".

Example from p. 29: Glow	Grow
In this column, write down three things you admire about yourself.	In this column, write down how you can improve on those qualities.
1. Artist	1. Learn how to draw a turtle.
2. Great Friend	2. Be a better listener. Don't interrupt my friends when they are talking.
3. Basketball Player	3. Make 7 out of 10 of my free throws.

Glow	Grow
In this column, write down three things you admire about yourself.	In this column, write down how you can improve on those qualities.
1.	1.
2.	2.
3.	3.

JOYJOYJOY *Joy* JOYJOYJOY

- Pink and Lavender clouds in a sunrise.
- Bats.
- Cardinals (the birds, not the team) :p
- Coffee houses.
- The sun seeping through a canopy of trees.
- Creeks.
- Lucille Ball.
- Morgan Freeman's voice.
- My Mamaw being sassy.
- Stars and telescopes.
- Dogs.
- BOOKS!
- Caves and biodiversity.
- Microscopes.
- Dancing.
- The color yellow.
- SCIENCE AND HISTORY!
- Flowers growing through a sidewalk.
- Butterflies and bees. <3 Well, all pollinators.
- Seeing the moon over the ocean.
- The sound leaves make in the fall beneath your feet.
- Alpacas.
- Bob Ross.
- Hobby Lobby

A note from Destany –

List random things that bring you joy. Write them out, or draw them in the space below.

Tag me in your list! #JourneywithDestany

RANDOM THINGS THAT BRING ME JOY

KEY RELATIONSHIPS

- This is not my own idea. This activity is from RUBY PAYNE'S Emotional Poverty, page 150.

A note from Destany –
One of the hardest lessons for me to learn was not everyone wishes you well. Some people hope you will fail because it makes them feel better about their shortcomings. These people do not deserve your time or energy. Maintain kindness always. However, it is essential you set personal boundaries.

ACTIVITY

Directions for Key Relationships chart on next page:

1. You are in the inner circle. In the other circles write the names of the people in your life, starting with the closest: Family, relatives & friends.

2. Draw a solid line to the people who support you in doing what you want to do.

3. Draw a dashed line to the people who will support you some of the time.

4. If a person does not support you, then draw no line.

5. Think about how you will deal with the people who do not support you. These are the people who slow you down or keep you from accomplishing your goals.

6. Talk to a trusted adult about how to deal with people who do not support you.

Thoughts:
_____
_____
_____
_____
_____
_____
_____
_____

Mamaw & Papaw

Sharon

Loving, adventurous, kind, free spirit
Daughter of Vada and H.D. (Henry Delmer)
Lover of her family
Who feels you should do your bucket list while you're young,
"DON'T WAIT!"
Who needs a miracle
Who gives support
Who fears nothing
Who would like to see The Grand Canyon
Resident of Missouri
Davis, Turrentine

Henry

Strong, brave, giving, kind
Son of Loran and Sarah
Lover of westerns
Who feels we should look to God for direction
Who needs Mamaw's cooking
Who gives life lessons
Who fears nothing
Who would like to see Montana become his home state
Resident of Missouri
Turrentine

ACTIVITY

Directions:

Make your own bio poem on the next page! Choose someone that you look up to or that inspires you. After you finish your poem, write it out on a separate piece of paper. For fun, decorate the poem with things that person loves. If possible, give it to them as a surprise.

BIO POEM

Explanation	Template/ Sentence Starter	Your Poem
Write their name.	Name	
Use four words that describe them.	4 Adjectives (Describer words)	
What do they love?	Lover of	
What do they feel?	Who feels	
What do they need?	Who needs	
What do they give to others?	Who gives	
What are they afraid of?	Who fears	
Where do they live?	Resident of	
Write their last name.	Last Name	

Procedural Self-Talk

This is Isaac. He had to use procedural self-talk when navigating obstacles in this cave.

Procedural self-talk is the way you talk yourself through a task. It is essential to have this skill to be successful in life.

You can practice this skill by "talking yourself" through cleaning your room. You may even want to make a checklist so that you visibly see how close you are to completing your task.

If you struggle with completing school assignments, ask your teacher for a checklist of the steps you need to complete it.

★ The most important part of practicing this skill is to complete the task.

CLEAN MY ROOM CHECKLIST

- ☐ CLEAN OFF DRESSER
- ☐ PICK UP BOOKS
- ☐ PUT DIRTY CLOTHES IN LAUNDRY
- ☐ PUT AWAY CLEAN CLOTHES
- ☐ MAKE BED
- ☐ PUT AWAY SHOES AND SOCKS
- ☐ THROW AWAY ANY GARBAGE
- ☐ Take dirty dishes to the kitchen (Including all the cups)

ACTIVITY

Practice procedural self-talk by completing the list above while cleaning your room. Remember to talk yourself through the task. The conversation may sound like this:

"First I will clean off my dresser."
"Okay I finished that. Awesome!"
"Next, I will pick up my books."
So on, and so forth. :) <u>Now you try!</u>

EXERCISE

Physical exercise is important for not only physical health, but also for our mental health.

A note from Destany –

In fifth grade I asked my mom if I could join a dance class. Instead, she signed Felisha and me up for Taekwondo. As it turned out, I learned something very important about myself in those classes in Marysville, California.

In my first sparring match, I kicked a boy in the left side of his stomach and sent him to the floor gasping for air. I apologized over and over again. He had a much higher belt than I did. In fact, if it were a video game, I would have been on level zero. I tried to help him up. He ignored me and said, "Don't apologize." He was embarrassed a little girl got a hit in on him.

I learned I hated fighting. However, I had no problem hitting the punching bag. Likewise, I loved the level of fitness that the course required. My instructor also stressed that the point of learning to fight is to avoid violence. I learned how to block punches and kicks. I also learned how to use a person's weight against them. I ended up really enjoying Taekwondo.

We left before I could advance in belts, but I did have fun.

ACTIVITY

Spell out your name, then do the exercises that match your letters.

A	10 jumping jacks	N	10 sit ups
B	10 squats	O	5 wind mills
C	5 crunches	P	10 burpees
D	10 push ups	Q	10 toe touches
E	10 wind mills	R	10 Russian twists
F	30 second run in place	S	1 minute wall sit
G	30 second mountain climbers	T	20 air punches
H	10 jump in place	U	10 lunges
I	30 second wall sit	V	30 second inch worms
J	10 jump ropes	W	10 burpees
K	5 push ups	X	20 high knees
L	10 fire hydrants	Y	30 second plank
M	20 high knees	Z	10 toe touches

Routines

Here is an example of a daily checklist. Feel free to use this one, or create your own! :)

A note from Destany –

Did you know having a daily routine can help reduce stress?

41

800-METER STATE CHAMPION

In 2011, I won the state championship in the 800-meter dash. The 800-meter dash is two laps around the track. It requires both speed and stamina. The race was held in the Acorn school district. They lined each of us up, and I was in the sixth lane. That means when they staggered us, I was the furthest back. I was going to have to hustle to break into the first lane.

"Racers on your mark, get set, *BOOM!*" The gunshot sounded.

I sprinted the around the curve and broke in on the first lane. I started passing girls. By the second curve I was in third place. I stayed there the entire first lap. I could hear the patter of feet against the track directly behind me. I picked up the pace. By the second lap in the first curve I moved to second place. I stayed behind the girl in second place letting her be my windbreak. At the last curve, I started a full sprint. My feet pounded against the turf. I leaned into my run just slightly. I continued the full sprint for the remaining 100 meters. When I crossed the finish line, my coach rushed up to me. He patted me on the back and said, "You're a state champion D!"

It was awesome to win a state championship! However, I'm telling this story because I didn't start out winning first place every time. In fact, there were events that I came in last. I had to learn how to pace myself. I also had to figure out how to control my breathing. It took time, but I have a trunk full of ribbons from competing in track. I'm proud of them all. It's proof I never stopped trying.

ACTIVITY
I challenge you to try a new hobby. Use the hashtag #journeywithdestany

Here is a list of ideas to choose from to help get you started.

- Painting
- Magic
- Cooking
- Birdwatching
- Creative Writing
- Volunteering (talk with a teacher to help get you started)
- Origami
- Reading
- Puzzle
- Chess
- Gardening

⇒ GRATITUDE ⇐

Once a week, challenge yourself to write down something for which you are grateful. Be specific in what you write. Don't just write, "I'm thankful for family and friends."

NOT SPECIFIC	SPECIFIC
"I'm thankful for my mom."	"Mom knew I didn't like what we were having at school for lunch today, so she packed me a lunch to take to school!"

Over time, what will happen is that your brain will continuously seek to find the good in situations.

For example:

One of the worst places that people try to force gratitude is when we experience tragedy.

Often statements are said to the victim like this, "It could be worse. You should be grateful that you don't have it as bad as so and so."

Please know there is a time and place for gratitude.
Also, you are smart and capable. Your feelings are valid.

Mary Nolan

On August 14th, 2015, I had the awesome privilege of flying with Mary Nolan. She is in the flying hall of fame! In addition, she is a five-time gold medalist aerobatic flier. She is a modern-day Amelia Earhart!

Ben, my husband, was building an airplane hangar for Mary, and knowing that becoming a pilot was a dream of mine, he told me about her. I asked him to inquire about how much she would charge to take me on a flight in her airplane. When he did, she instructed him to have me come to the hangar immediately and that she would take me up! Upon arrival, she introduced herself and informed me that she would NOT accept a payment.

This was a flight of my wildest dreams. We were in a taildragger, which is an aircraft capable of aerobatic maneuvers. The plane was mostly white, except for the two red stripes straight down the middle.

Her husband helped her preflight the plane, then Mary and I climbed in. There was room for two people total. The pilot seat was directly in front of the passenger seat, so I sat in the back. However, there was a yoke in the back with me as well. The yoke controls the up and down motion of an aircraft, and rolling it left or right. After I buckled up, she handed me a headset.

"Do you like rollercoasters?" Mary asked.

"Not really, I'm terrified of them," I replied.

With a smile, Mary handed me a brown paper bag. She chuckled, "You might need this in case you get sick."

I took the bag and set it beside me. Up until she handed me the bag, I thought this was going to be an ordinary flight. I assumed we would take-off, make a pattern, and then land.

What came next was the most exciting experience of my life. We taxied to the end of the grass strip in the plane. As soon as we were facing straight, she gave the plane full throttle. We zoomed down the runway. At the end of the runway was a row of pine trees. We kept getting closer and closer. I looked out my window and saw every single wheel still on the ground. We weren't even hovering. I knew at the speed we were going we would surely crash into the tree line.

Just as we were about to meet our doom, she pulled back on the yoke and we went straight up into the air. I felt as if an immense force weighed me down and an unseen hand was holding me back in my seat. Then, she leveled off and the weight went away.

What I had just experienced is called a g-force. Right now, you are currently experiencing one-G. A g-force is gravity holding you down. G-forces can increase as an object is accelerated. For example, a person experiencing 2 g weighs twice their normal weight. So, if someone weighs 150lbs at 2 g they would feel the weight of 300 pounds. That is the heaviness I was experiencing, and I LOVED IT!

That abrupt take off was only the beginning. Next, Mary did a barrel roll! It is a single turn of a spiral. This means we did a flip in the air! After every maneuver, Mary would level off in steady flight and ask how I felt. Then, she would ask me what I thought of the stunt.

I'm sure she believes the only word in my vocabulary is amazing! It was the single word I could give. I said it over and over during our flight. It was an experience beyond words. Nothing could capture the joy and fulfillment provided to me in this moment, and it was nowhere near over. We flew upside down, completed steep turns, and did a few other stunts. Right before she brought the plane down, she asked me if I wanted to fly. Of course, I did!

Following her instruction, I made small turns and changed our elevation.

While I was flying, I experienced a moment of stillness. It was as if I was seeing things in slow motion. It was a peace that surrounded me and filled my heart with joy. Years of watching birds in flight, pausing to catch glimpses of airplanes passing over, dreams of having wings, and now this – I was meant to become a pilot.

I made a plan to make becoming a pilot a reality. It took six years to save up enough money, but I was successful.

ACTIVITY

Think of a time in your life that someone did something special for you. What did they do? How did you feel at that moment? Describe that experience below.

What is something special you could do for someone else?

Thoughts:

_____

_____

_____

_____

_____

_____

_____

_____

Cardboard Boat Races

July 30th, 2016
Location: HEBER SPRINGS, ARKANSAS

Water laps against the bank of the lake. The sun transforms the ripples into a sea of diamonds. It's so bright we all must wear our shades. There are boats in every direction as far as the eyes can see. It is the 2016 Annual Cardboard boat races held at Greer's Ferry Lake in Heber Springs, Arkansas.

Arkansas State University (ASU) Heber Springs asked Larone Lowe and me to race the boat for the college that year. We shared a class together at ASU and were good friends. It is tradition for ASU students to captain the boat. The boat was fashioned together by their engineering students. It is solid white, except for the decks that are trimmed with blue duct tape. On the right resides the ASU logo.

The boats were extraordinary. They were of every design that you could imagine. One boat looked like the house from the Disney movie, UP. Another boat looked like a giant red parrot laying on its back, and it could hold up to six men.

The only materials allowed to be used to build the boats are cardboard and duct tape, so many of the them quickly sank when they touched the water. Our boat stood out for its simplicity. However, our boat had something very special... its history. It was known by everyone because it has been in several races and had survived each one.

The announcer gave us the call for the heat races. Only the racers with the fastest times would move on to compete in the main event.

Larone and I steadied the boat in the water. I will never forget the giant swan boat on our left side. The swan lay on its back and its wings stretched far out to the sides. It was as if it was getting ready to give a hug to the captain when he stepped in the middle of it at the last second. As soon as they signaled for us to go, he jumped in his boat and it quickly began to sink. Several of the boats around us were going under.

I tried to stay focused. I was positioned in the front of the boat and Larone was in the back. I knew being paired with slow boats wasn't good. It's just like in track and field. You want to race with the fastest heat because it will push you to do your best. It is easy to go slower if there is no competition.

I paddled as fast as I could. When our boat would veer off to the side, Larone would correct it with his paddle and steady our course. We finished first in our heat with ease. We would have to wait and see if we made the finals.

A few hours later, they called our names and our boat. We were in the finals! We were competing with a small group.

Our biggest competition would be another canoe. The keel (or front) of the canoe came to a thin point. It allowed them to soar through the water with ease. They also didn't teeter back and forth when they paddled.

We all lined up our boats. We checked our life jackets then climbed into the boat. A gunshot signaled the race had started. Again, we paddled as fast as we could.

We managed to pass several boats by the midway point and we were in second place!

All at once, Larone's paddle broke off! All that was left was a pole. He started using his hands on the sides and I paddled all I could. We still managed to finish third in the World Champion Cardboard Boat Races with a broken paddle! It was so much fun!

ACTIVITY

Look up the Cardboard Boat Races in Heber Springs, Arkansas.
If you are not able to compete, go on out and enjoy the show.
The boats will dazzle you!

Thoughts:
_____
_____
_____
_____

WILD CAVE TOUR

The morning of the Wild Cave Tour we showed up thirty minutes before our arrival time. When we approached the building, the front doors were still locked. I looked up to see a balcony, and at the top was a young forest service employee. He hurried down the stairs, unlocked the door, and let us in.

D.J., as he introduced himself, was a wonderful person. He told us jokes, gave us a rundown of what to expect on the tour, and told us to make ourselves at home. Although originally supposed to be our guide, he was being pulled from the schedule to help work in recreation. Our guide today would be someone named Paul.

We were lounging in the lobby when Paul came down the stairs wearing a green pair of coveralls. He was geared with a helmet, caving pack, and boots. I didn't know it at the time, but Paul McIntosh would become one of my dearest friends.

"Are you the wild cavers?" he asked.

"Yes!" we replied.

"I thought so!" he exclaimed. "Have you been on the Wild Tour before?"

"We haven't!"

"Me, either!" Paul said. "This should be fun!"

Paul made this statement without even a slight chuckle to give us the intimation he was joking, but he clearly was. We all busted out laughing. In the first minute of our meeting he had set the tone of the tour. It was full of fun and laughter.

Once we were all geared up, we took a short bus ride to the man-made exit, which served as our entrance to the Wild Cave Tour.

We followed the sidewalk trail until it came to a railing. At this point, we stepped off the pavement and onto the clay. It was like entering another world. The remainder of the tour was completely undeveloped. We crawled over breakdown, and walked beneath cave chandeliers and curtains.

I was so close to the stalactites, I could see the crystal structures inside the droplets of water that hugged the formation. When the light touched the formations the crystal faces would reflect the light back. We were surrounded by crystals!

Once we reached our lunch-time destination, I was in the presence of an 85-foot tall pure white stalagmite. A single drip formation will grow one cubic square inch per one hundred years. The formations that I got to stand next to were there before my name was called into existence and will remain there long after I am gone.

I had an overwhelming sense of smallness and a greater value of time. Every second that I spent in the cave, I knew I was meant to be there.

The wonders were just beginning! Throughout our tour, Paul would quiz us on where we were in the cave. He would take us back to the same room and ask me what I would find if I ventured a certain direction. No matter how hard he tried, he couldn't stump me.

During parts of the tour, Paul had allowed me to be what is called a trail guide. When Kelly and her friend would traverse a path, I helped Paul with the safety positions. I also helped encourage our team when completing a course to get to the next destination.

Three-quarters of the way through the tour, we had reached a ledge that is mounded over with slick clay. The ledge that is walked on is shaped like a Razorback, which is how it earned its name. To get across the hiker sticks their hand into a small crevice on the wall nearest the razor back. Then, they must scissor walk across it. At the end, they will climb down a five-foot drop to a small canyon.

While helping my group across the Razorback, Paul asked if I would like a job at Blanchard Springs Caverns. Of course, I said yes! He told me all about how to apply. It turns out that my tour guide was also a supervisor at Blanchard.

The following summer I was hired at Blanchard Springs Caverns. I made lifelong friends with many of the tour guides. It also led to future opportunities in caving adventures.

ACTIVITY

What is an activity you have always dreamed of doing?

Where would you go?

Who would you take with you?

Spiritual Resource

Whether it is meditation, mindfulness, or prayer – these things aid us in emotional stability.

Perhaps one of my favorite things about caving is when I go and sit in a room alone. I only do this close to the entrance in what cavers call the twilight zone. I'm on the edge of darkness, but I can still see the light. I will sit in complete silence and meditate.

I immediately become aware of the fact that silence is loud. I hear the creek churning as it passes by formations. I hear the soft fluttering of bat wings. I hear the dripping of water on rocks. I notice how the clay that rests on the cave floor creates an earthy smell.

Then, I become aware of my own heart-beat. I notice my shoulders move slightly upwards when I take a deep breath, and how they fall when I exhale.

This is mindfulness. I only pay attention to the moment that I am currently in.

ACTIVITY

MINDFULNESS
Don't think about what happened in the past. Don't imagine the future.
<u>I want you to focus on this current moment.</u>

Revisit this page as often as you like, or as you need it. It uses the five senses to help you think about what you are experiencing in the current moment. You can write your response down, say them out loud, or even think of them silently to yourself. :)

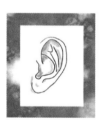    

Right now, I hear...	Right now, I see...	Right now, I smell...	Right now, I feel...	Right now, I am touching...

BOULDERING

In 2021, Blanchard Springs Caverns hosted a bouldering competition. Corey, a professional climber, organized the event. There was a small crowd of men setting up pads that the participants would land on after completing a climb. I talked with two of the rangers who were working the event. They are also friends of mine, Trey and Aaron. They informed me this was the very first climbing event in Blanchard history. I turned to Ben, my husband, and told him I wanted to join the event. He laughed, completely unsurprised by my response.

As if on cue, Corey came over and asked if I wanted to join the competition. I was wearing blue jeans and tennis shoes. I really wasn't dressed for the event. I told Corey I wanted to compete, and asked if it was okay if I wore the shoes I had. He walked me over to a tote that had mounds of climbing shoes. "Here, use one of these! I always have them just in case."

"Thanks!" I said.

I picked out a pair of shoes. A man with Corey gave me a chalk bag, and just like that, I was in the competition. I had no clue what the rules were. I quickly learned it was harder than it first appeared. For starters, a climb must begin in a seated position with both feet touching the cliff, then the climber would have to pull themselves up. It required an extreme amount of arm strength. The next rule I learned is that both hands had to touch the piece of tape at the peak of the course to complete the climb. Once the climber reached that point, then they would drop to the mats. Climbers had three attempts at a course for it to score.

The first and second courses I finished with ease. At the third course I began to struggle. I had to maintain a left-hand hold with just two fingers, keep my toes on a sliver of rock, lean down and reach with my right hand. I stretched out my right hand toward the tape. I was almost there!

As soon as my hand touched the tape, my left foot slipped and I fell. I slammed hard on the mat. I had two more attempts. I fell two more times. I knew it didn't count, but I asked Corey if I could complete the course. He said that would be fine because they had plenty of mats so I wasn't holding anyone up. I started climbing again. Slam! I hit the pad again. I got back up. By my seventh attempt the climbers were gathered around me. One of them turned to Ben, "Man, she doesn't give up, does she?"

"No, she's pretty headstrong," Ben said.

The climbers started coaching me. They showed me how to sit in a hold. On my tenth attempt I had a good hold with my right hand and was just about to get my left hand to latch on, then I fell.

It took me twelve times before I finally managed to complete the course! When both hands latched on to that piece of tape my arms were shaking! I held it then let go. The other climbers applauded. It was awesome!

I didn't win. However, I think it is important to try new things for the fun of it! Usually, people don't start out amazing straight out the gate. Give yourself time to learn and grow. I went home that day and ordered myself a chalk bag, a pair of climbing shoes, and a mat. It is now one of my new hobbies.

ACTIVITY

What do you do for fun? How did you get started in this hobby?

Thoughts:

_____

_____

_____

_____

_____

_____

_____

Do me a favor. Think about how old you are right now. Now add sixteen years to it. How old would you be? Imagine waiting sixteen years before you could start a goal. That is exactly what happened to me. I knew at the age of ten I wanted to become a pilot recreationally. I would dream of flying all the time. During the day, I would stop to observe airplanes flying overhead. In my dreams, I could just lift one foot, then the other, and roll onto the air. I would soar above treetops and waterfalls.

My senior year of high school I learned how expensive it was to become a pilot. It was definitely outside my means, financially. That didn't stop me from talking to every pilot with which I came into contact. I would quiz them on how they became a pilot, what flight school they attended, and what advice they would give someone who wanted to become a pilot.

Finally, in 2020, I made a decision on which flight school I would attend. I chose a Part 61 school. The year before I was to start my lessons, I purchased a private pilot starter kit. I spent that year studying those materials. I worked three jobs and saved money. As soon as I would get a large sum saved, an emergency would happen and I would have to start saving all over again. In addition to struggling financially, I had several people tell me it was a waste of time. They questioned why I intended on being a pilot, when I was already a teacher.

But on June 3rd, 2021, my dreams became a reality. I took my first flight lesson. The clouds were my playground. I understood complete JOY. It was the sweetest kind that can only be achieved after hard work.

This is probably one of the most important things I will share with you. The things that excite you, the ideas and dreams that give you butterflies, those are the very things you should pursue full force. The best part is that it does not need to make sense to anyone but you.

Remember, YOU CAN DO ANYTHING if you are willing to work for it!

Tag me in your homemade piggy banks! #journeywithdestany

Make your own piggy bank and start saving money for something you want.

You can use any container from the grocery store, a cleaned-up paper coffee cup from the coffee shop, or even a can.

- Did you know you can put money in a bank now while you're young and it collects interest? That means they pay you to have money in the bank! This is something I wish I would have known about as a child.

- Consider asking your family about opening your own savings account! You can put money away to save so you won't be able to access until you're 18. Then you could even buy your own car, boat, four-wheeler, pay for college, or make a down payment on a house! Talk with your local banker for more information.

Thoughts:

_____

_____

_____

_____

_____

_____

_____

_____

_____

_____

_____

_____

_____

_____

_____

_____

_____

_____

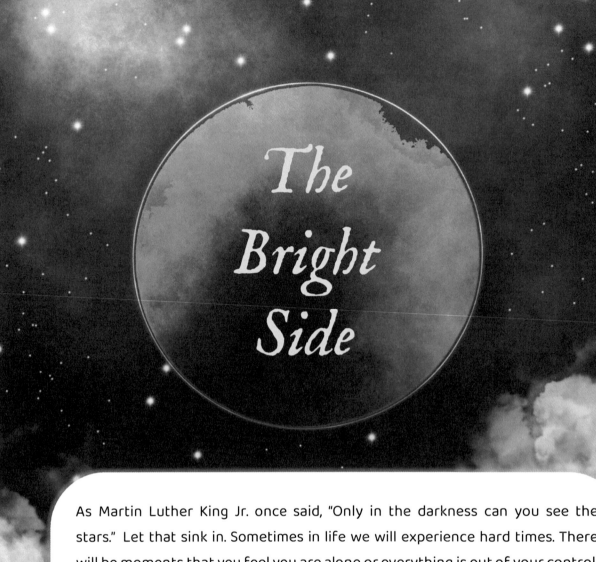

The Bright Side

As Martin Luther King Jr. once said, "Only in the darkness can you see the stars." Let that sink in. Sometimes in life we will experience hard times. There will be moments that you feel you are alone or everything is out of your control. I want you to remember there are always people who support you and who are on your side. This world is lucky to have you and it is a better place because you exist. Hard times will come, but remember, they are temporary. So, when you are surrounded in darkness, lean on your supporters, and look to the stars. The bright side is what you carry inside you. It is the knowledge that you overcome past obstacles, therefore you are capable of making it through any future tribulations. Be kind to others. You are incredibly loved. Wishing you many happy adventures in life!   - Destany Lytle

Acknowledgements

A special thanks to my publishers, Suzanne and James Babb, for their time and expertise. Suzanne paid every attention to detail. From the artistic titles, to the firefly located by each page number, she brought my dreams for this book to life. James edited the text with careful eyes ensuring the best quality of the story was presented. Without these two amazing people I surely would have been lost in the pursuit of publishing this book.

Furthermore, my special gratitude goes out to Ruby Payne. Her research and writing enlightened me as an educator. It imprinted on all facets of my life, particularly in the way I communicate and work with others. Her research inspired me to write this book. As a child from both generational and emotional poverty, I find her work to be a blueprint to making a life changing difference for children.

In addition, I would like to thank my family. To the Standard, the Turrentine, and the Lytle family, your love and support means the world to me. I love you!

Lastly, I would like to thank my loving husband, Ben, for his eagerness to listen to my stories and ideas. He is always ready to join me on my next adventure!

About the Author

DESTANY LYTLE is a proud Arkansas educator. She teaches Social Studies at Midland Elementary. When she is not teaching, she can be found 216 feet underground at Blanchard Springs Caverns! In the summers you can almost always find her leading tours. Kids and caves are her world, and she loves sharing it with children in her book, *A Cave Adventure.* In addition, Destany is a member of the National Speleological Society (a group that studies caves.)

Destany currently resides in Arkansas and is pursuing her pilot license.

Made in the USA
Coppell, TX
16 February 2023